In the
of Angels

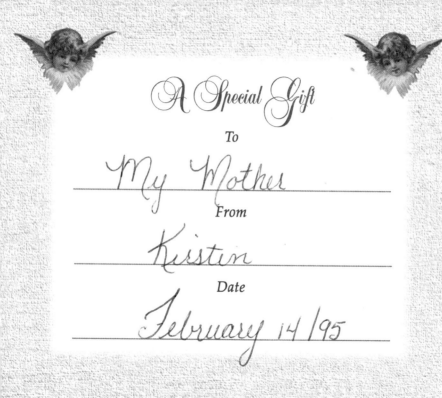

A Special Gift

To

My Mother

From

Kristen

Date

February 14 /95

Ribbons of Love

GARDENS OF FRIENDSHIP

HAPPY IS THE HOUSE
That Shelters a Friend

IN THE PRESENCE OF ANGELS

JUST FOR YOU:
A Celebration of Joy and Friendship

LOVING THOUGHTS
for Tender Hearts

MOTHER
Another Word for Love

In the Presence of Angels

of Angels

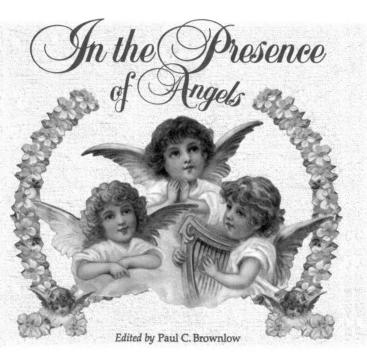

Edited by Paul C. Brownlow

Brownlow Publishing Company, Inc.

O passing Angel, speed me with a song,
A melody of heaven to reach my heart
And rouse me to the race and
make me strong.

CHRISTINA ROSSETTI

It is wonderful that every angel, in whatever direction he turns his body and face, sees the Lord in front of him.

EMANUEL SWEDENBORG

If there is anything that keeps the mind open to angel visits, and repels the ministry to evil, it is a pure human love.

N. P. WILLIS

See that you do not look down on one of these little ones. For I tell you that their angels in heaven always see the face of my Father in heaven.

MATTHEW 18:10

Our lives are albums written through with good or ill, with false or true; and as the blessed angels turn the pages of our years, God grant they read the good with smiles, and blot the ill with tears!

JOHN GREENLEAF WHITTIER

*Remember though thy foes are strong
and tried, the angels of Heaven are on
thy side, and God is over all!*

ADELAIDE A. PROCTER

*Go with me, like good angels, to my end;
And, as the long divorce of steel falls on me,
Make of your prayers one sweet sacrifice,
And lift my soul to heaven.*

WILLIAM SHAKESPEARE

Angels at Creation

Where were you when I laid the earth's foundation? Tell me, if you understand. Who marked off its dimensions? Surely you know! Who stretched a measuring line across it? On what were its footings set, or who laid its cornerstone—while the morning stars sang together and all the angels shouted for joy?

JOB 38:4-7

The Ministry of Angels

And is there care in Heaven? And is there love
In heavenly spirits to these creatures base,
That may compassion of their evils move?
There is:—else much more wretched were the case
Of men than beasts: but O! th' exceeding grace
Of highest God, that loves his creatures so,
And all his works with mercy doth embrace,
That blessed angels he sends to and fro,
To serve to wicked man, to serve his foe!

How oft do they their silver bowers leave
To come to succor us that succor want!
How oft do they with golden pinions cleave
The flitting skies, like flying pursuivant,
Against foul fiends to aid us militant!
They for us fight, they watch and duly ward,
And their bright squadrons round about us
plant;
And all for love, and nothing for reward:
O! why should heavenly God to men
have such regard?

EDMUND SPENCER

Cherubim, seraphim, all the angelic host
as they are described in Scripture,
have a wild and radiant power that
often takes us by surprise. They are not
always gentle. They bar the entrance
to Eden, so that we may never return home.
They send plagues upon the Egyptians.
They are messengers of God. They are winds.
They are flames of fire. They are
young men dressed in white.

MADELEINE L'ENGLE

How like an angel came I down!
How bright are all things here!
When first among his works I did appear,
Oh, how their glory did me crown!

THOMAS TRAHERNE

To comfort and to bless,
To find a balm for woe,
To tend the lone and fatherless,
Is angels' work below.

W. W. HOW

Listening Angels

When the chant was done, and lingering
Died upon the evening air,
From the hill the radiant Angels
Still were listening there.

Silent came the gathering darkness,
Bringing with it sleep and rest;
Save a little bird was singing
Near her leafy nest.

Through the sounds of war and labor
She had warbled all day long,
While the Angels leant and listened
Only to her song.

But the starry night was coming;
When she ceased her little lay,
From the mountaintop the Angels
Slowly passed away.

ADELAIDE A. PROCTER

*How shall we tell an angel from another
guest? How, from the common worldly herd,
one of the blest?*

*Hint of suppressed halo, rustle of hidden wings,
wafture of heavenly frankincense,
—which is these things?*

*The old Sphinx smiles so subtly:
"I give no golden rule,—yet I would warn thee,
world: treat well whom thou call'st fool."*

GERTRUDE HALL

Angels mean messengers and ministers.
Their function is to execute the plan
of divine providence, even in earthly things.

THOMAS AQUINAS

The stars shine on brightly while Adam
and Eve pursue their way into the far
wilderness. There is a sound through the
silence, as of the falling tears of an angel.

ELIZABETH BARRETT BROWNING

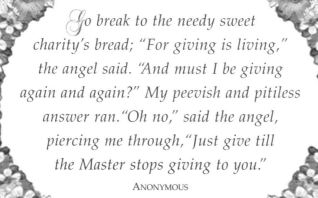

Go break to the needy sweet charity's bread; "For giving is living," the angel said. "And must I be giving again and again?" My peevish and pitiless answer ran. "Oh no," said the angel, piercing me through, "Just give till the Master stops giving to you."

ANONYMOUS

*Over all our tears God's
rainbow bends, to all our cries a
pitying ear He lends;
yea, to the feeble sounds
of man's lament, how often have
His messengers been sent!*

CAROLINE NORTON

Angels Ahead

*See, I am sending an angel ahead of you
to guard you along the way and
to bring you to the place I have prepared.
Pay attention to him and listen
to what he says. Do not rebel against
him; he will not forgive your
rebellion, since my Name is in him.*

EXODUS 23:20-21

Angels guard you when you walk with God.
What better way could you choose?

FRANCES J. ROBERTS

Every breath of air and ray of light and heat,
every beautiful prospect, is, as it were,
the skirts of their garments, the weaving of
the robes of those whose faces see God.

JOHN HENRY NEWMAN

Ring out ye crystal spheres,
Once bless our human ears
(If ye have power to touch our senses so)
And let your silver chime
Move in melodious time;
And let the base of heav'n's deep organ blow,
And with your ninefold harmony
Make up full consort to th' angelic symphony.

JOHN MILTON

And now it is an angel's song,
That makes the heavens be mute.

SAMUEL TAYLOR COLERIDGE

An angel stood and met my gaze,
through the low doorway of my tent;
the tent is struck, the vision stays;
—I only know she came and went.

JAMES RUSSELL LOWELL

Ministering Angels

*Angels of light, spread your bright wings
and keep near me at morn: nor in the starry eve,
nor midnight deep, leave me forlorn. From all
dark spirits of unholy power guard my weak heart,
circle around me in each perilous hour,
and take my part.*

*From all foreboding thoughts and dangerous
fears, keep me secure; teach me to hope,
and through the bitterest tears still to endure.*

UNKNOWN

*If lonely in the road so fair and wide my feet
should stray, then through a rougher, safer
pathway guide me day by day. Should my heart
faint at its unequal strife, O still be near! Shadow
the perilous sweetness of this life with holy fear.*

*Then leave me not alone in this bleak world,
where'er I roam, and at the end, with your bright
wings unfurled, O take me home!*

ADELAIDE A. PROCTER

*At the round earth's imagin'd corners,
blow your trumpets, angels, and
arise, arise from death, you numberless
infinities of souls.*

JOHN DONNE

How sweetly did they float upon the wings
Of silence through the empty-vaulted night,
At every fall smoothing the raven down
Of darkness till it smiled!

JOHN MILTON

They are idols of hearts and of households;
They are angels of God in disguise;
The sunlight that sleeps in their tresses,
His glory still gleams in their eyes;
These truants from home and from Heaven,
They have made me more manly and mild;
And I know now how Jesus could liken
The kingdom of God to a child.

CHARLES MONROE DICKINSON

The Touch of the Angel's Hand

Life is so generous a giver, but we, judging its gifts by their covering, cast them away as ugly, or heavy, or hard. Remove the covering, and you will find beneath it, a living splendor, woven of love, by wisdom, with power.

Welcome it, grasp it, and you touch the angel's hand that brings it to you. Everything we call a trial, a sorrow, or a duty, believe me, that angel's hand is there.

FRA GIOVANNI

Hallelujah! Praise Jehovah!

Hallelujah! Praise Jehovah!
From the heavens! praise His name;
Praise Jehovah in the highest;
All His angels praise proclaim,
All His hosts together praise Him,
Sun and moon and stars on high;
Praise Him, O ye heaven of heavens,
And ye floods above the sky.

FROM PSALM 148

Angelic Chorus

All the angels were standing around the throne
and around the elders and the four living
creatures. They fell down on their faces
before the throne and worshiped God, saying:

"Amen! Praise and glory
and wisdom and thanks and honor
and power and strength
be to our God for ever and ever. Amen!"

REVELATION 7:11-12

Millions of spiritual creatures walk the earth unseen, both when we wake, and when we sleep: all these with ceaseless praise his works behold both day and night.

JOHN MILTON

Come, let us join our cheerful songs
With angels round the throne;
Ten thousand thousand are their tongues,
But all their joys are one.

ISAAC WATTS

Prayer

I asked for bread; God gave a stone instead.
Yet, while I pillowed there my weary head,
The angels made a ladder of my dreams,
Which upward to celestial mountains led.
And when I woke beneath the morning's beams,
Around my resting place fresh manna lay;
And, praising God, I went upon my way.
For I was fed.

God answers prayer; sometimes,
When hearts are weak,
He gives the very gifts believers seek.
But often faith must learn a deeper rest,
And trust God's silence when He does not speak;
For He whose name is Love will send the best.
Stars may burn out, nor mountain walls endure,
But God is true, His promises are sure
For those who seek.

AUTHOR UNKNOWN

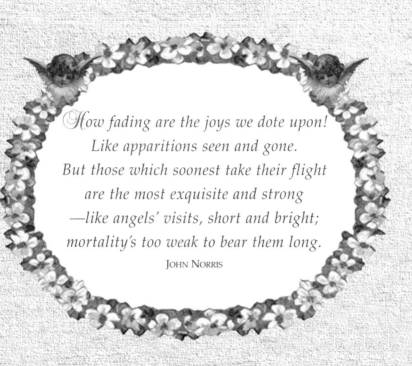

How fading are the joys we dote upon!
Like apparitions seen and gone.
But those which soonest take their flight
are the most exquisite and strong
—like angels' visits, short and bright;
mortality's too weak to bear them long.

JOHN NORRIS

Speak ye who best can tell, ye sons of light,

Angels, for ye behold him, and with songs

And choral symphonies, day without night,

Circle his throne rejoicing.

JOHN MILTON

Little Bell

"What good child is this," the angel said,
"that, with happy heart, beside her bed prays
so lovingly?" Low and soft, oh! very low and soft,
crooned the blackbird in the orchard croft,
"Bell, dear Bell!" crooned he. "Whom God's
creatures love," the angel fair murmured,
"God doth bless with angels' care: child, thy
bed shall be folded safe from harm. Love, deep
and kind, shall watch around, and leave good
gifts behind, Little Bell, for thee."

THOMAS WESTWOOD

Although I'm Not an Angel

So, although I'm not an angel,
yet I know that over there
I will join the blessed chorus
that the angels cannot share;
I will sing about my Saviour,
who upon dark Calvary
Freely pardoned my transgressions,
died to set a sinner free.

JOHNSON OATMAN

When we survey Almighty God surrounded
by his holy angels, his thousand thousands
of ministering spirits, and ten thousand times ten
thousand standing before him, the idea of his
awful majesty rises before us more powerfully and
impressively. We begin to see how little we are,
how altogether mean and worthless

in ourselves, and how high he is and fearful.
The very lowest of his angels is indefinitely above
us in this our present state; how high, then,
must be the Lord of angels! The very seraphim hide
their faces before his glory, while they praise
him; how shamefaced, then, should sinners be when
they come into his presence!

JOHN HENRY NEWMAN

Ten Thousand Angels

Then I looked and heard the voice of
many angels, numbering thousands upon
thousands, and ten thousand times ten
thousand.... In a loud voice they sang:
"Worthy is the Lamb, who was slain, to receive
power and wealth and wisdom and strength
and honor and glory and praise!"

REVELATION 5:11-12

*Once in an age,
God sends to some of us a friend
who loves in us...not the person
that we are, but the angel we may be.*

HARRIET BEECHER STOWE

*An angel can illumine the thought and
mind of man by strengthening the power of
vision, and by bringing within his
reach some truth which the angel
himself contemplates.*

THOMAS AQUINAS

The Angels in the House

Three pairs of dimpled arms as white as snow
Held me in soft embrace;
Three little cheeks, like velvet peaches soft,
Were placed against my face.

Three pairs of tiny eyes, so clear, so deep,
Looked up in mine this even;
Three pairs of lips kissed me a sweet "Good night,"
Three little forms from Heaven.

Ah, it is well that "little ones" should love us;
It lights our faith when dim,

To know that once our blessed Saviour bade them
Bring "little ones" to him.

And said he not, "Of such is Heaven," and
blessed them,
And held them to his breast?
Is it not sweet to know that, when they leave us,
'Tis then they go to rest?

And yet, ye tiny angels of my house,
Three hearts encased in mine,
How 'twould be shattered if the Lord should say,
"Those angels are not thine!"

ANONYMOUS

One and One

Two little eyes to open and close,
Two little ears and one little nose,
Two little elbows, dimpled and sweet,
Two little shoes on two little feet,
Two little lips and one little chin,
Two little cheeks with a rose shut in;
Two little shoulders, chubby and strong,

Two little legs running all day long.
Two little prayers does my darling say,
Twice does he kneel by my side each day,—
Two little folded hands, soft and brown,
Two little eyelids cast meekly down,—
And two little angels guard him in bed,
"One at the foot, and one at the head."

MARY MAPES DODGE

Then, crowned again, their golden harps they took, harps ever tuned, that glittering by their side like quivers hung, and with preamble sweet of charming symphony they introduce their sacred song, and waken raptures high; no voice exempt, no voice but well could join melodious part, such concord is in heaven.

JOHN MILTON

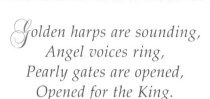

Golden harps are sounding,
Angel voices ring,
Pearly gates are opened,
Opened for the King.

FRANCES R. HAVERGAL

There are strange ways of serving God;
You sweep a room or turn a sod,
And suddenly, to your surprise,
You hear the whirr of seraphim,
And find you're under God's own eyes
And building palaces for Him.

HERMAN HAGEDORN

Who Is the Angel That Cometh?

I

Who is the Angel that cometh? Life! Let us not question what he brings, peace or strife. Under the shadow of his mighty wings, one by one, are his secrets told; one by one, lit by the rays of each morning sun, shall a new flower its petals unfold, with the mystery hid in its heart of gold.

We will arise and go forth to greet him, singly, gladly, with one accord;—"Blessed is he that cometh in the name of the Lord."

II

Who is the Angel that cometh? Joy!
Look at his glittering rainbow wings—
No alloy lies in the radiant gifts he brings;
tender and sweet, he is come to-day, tender
and sweet: while chains of love on his silver
feet will hold him in lingering fond delay. But
greet him quickly, he will not stay. Soon he
will
leave us; but though for others all his brightest
treasures are stored;—"Blessed is he that
cometh in the name of the Lord!"

III

Who is the Angel that cometh? Pain!
Let us arise and go forth to greet him;
Not in vain is the summons come for us to
meet him; he will stay, and darken our sun;
he will stay a desolate night, a weary day,
since in that shadow our work is done,
and in that shadow our crowns are won.
Let us say still, while his bitter chalice
slowly into our hearts is poured,—"Blessed is
he that cometh in the name of the Lord."

IV

Who is the Angel that cometh? Death!
But do not shudder and do not fear;
hold your breath, for a kingly presence is
drawing near. Cold and bright is his
flashing steel, cold and bright the smile that
comes like a starry light to calm the terror
and grief we feel; he comes to help and to save
and heal: then let us, baring our hearts
and kneeling, sing, while we wait this Angel's
sword,—"Blessed is he that cometh
in the name of the Lord!"

ADELAIDE ANNE PROCTER

And the wearied heart grew strong,
As an angel strengthened him,
Fainting in the garden dim
'Neath the world's vast woe and wrong.

JOHANN RIST

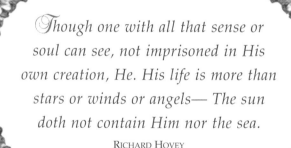

*Though one with all that sense or
soul can see, not imprisoned in His
own creation, He. His life is more than
stars or winds or angels— The sun
doth not contain Him nor the sea.*

RICHARD HOVEY

He Delivers Them

I will extol the Lord at all times; his praise will always be on my lips. My soul will boast in the Lord; let the afflicted hear and rejoice.

Glorify the Lord with me; Let us exalt his name together. I sought the Lord, and he answered me; he delivered me from all my fears.

Those who look to him are radiant;
their faces are never covered with shame.
This poor man called, and the Lord heard him;
he saved him out of all his troubles.
The angel of the Lord encamps around those
who fear him, and he delivers them.

PSALM 34:5-7

Still through the cloven skies they come,
With peaceful wings unfurled;
And still their heavenly music floats
O'er all the weary world;
Above its sad and lonely plains
They bend on hovering wing;
And o'er its Babel sounds
The blessed angels sing.

EDMUND HAMILTON SEARS

Better than beauty and than youth
Are saints and angels, a glad company.

DANTE GABRIEL ROSSETTI

The helmed Cherubim,
And sworded Seraphim,
Are seen in glittering ranks
with wings display'd.

JOHN MILTON

Sculptors of Life

Chisel in hand stood a sculptor boy
With his marble block before him,
And his eye lit up with a gleam of joy
When his life dream passed before him.

He carved it well on the shapeless stone
With many a sharp incision;
That angel dream he made his own,
His own that angel vision.

Sculptors of life are we as we stand
With our souls uncarved before us,
Waiting the time when at God's command
Our life dream shall pass o'er us.

If we carve it well on the shapeless stone,
With many a sharp incision,
That angel dream we make our own,
Our own that angel vision.

GEORGE W. DOANE

Rescued by an Angel

Then Nebuchadnezzar said, "Praise be to the God of Shadrach, Meshach and Abednego, who has sent his angel and rescued his servants! They trusted in him and defied the king's command and were willing to give up their lives rather than serve or worship any god except their own God."

DANIEL 3:28

For he will command his angels concerning you to guard you in all your ways; they will lift you up in their hands, so that you will not strike your foot against a stone.

PSALM 91:11-12

Good Company

Today I have grown taller from walking
with the trees, these seven sister-
poplars who go softly in a line; and I
think my heart is whiter for its parley
with a star that trembled out at
nightfall and hung above the pine.

The call-note of a redbird from the cedars
in the dusk woke his happy mate
within me to an answer free and fine;
and a sudden angel beckoned from
a column of blue smoke—Lord,
who am I that they should stoop
—these holy folk of thine?

KARLE WILSON BAKER

The Speech of Angels

Music is well said to be the speech of angels; in fact, nothing among the utterances allowed to man, is felt to be so Divine. It brings us near to the infinite; we look for moments across the cloudy elements into the eternal light,

when song leads and inspires us.
Serious nations, all nations that can listen
to the mandate of nature, have prized
song and music as a vehicle for worship,
for prophecy, and for whatsoever in
them was Divine.

THOMAS CARLYLE

*An angel is an intelligent essence,
always in motion. It has free will,
is incorporeal, serves God,
and has been bestowed with immortality.*

JOHN OF DAMASCUS

*It is in rugged crises,
in unweariable endurance,
and in aims which put sympathy
out of the question,
that the angel is shown.*

RALPH WALDO EMERSON

Our Mothers

O magical word, may it never die from the
lips that love to speak it,
Nor melt away from the trusting hearts
that even would break to keep it.

Was there ever a name that lived like thine!
Will there ever be another?
The angels have reared in heaven a shrine
to the holy name of Mother.

AUTHOR UNKNOWN

Love and Pity

God called the nearest angels who dwell with
Him above: the tenderest one was Pity,
the dearest one was Love.

"Arise," He said, "my angels! a wail of woe
and sin steals through the gates of heaven,
and saddens all within.

"My harps take up the mournful strain that from
a lost world swells, the smoke of torment clouds
the light and blights the asphodels.

"Fly downward to that under world,
and on its souls of pain let Love drop smiles
like sunshine, and Pity tears like rain!"
Two faces bowed before the Throne,
veiled in their golden hair; four white wings
lessened swiftly down the dark abyss of air.

The way was strange, the flight was
long; at last the angels came where swung
the lost and nether world, red-wrapped
in rayless flame.

There Pity, shuddering, wept; but Love, with faith too strong for fear, took heart from God's almightiness and smiled a smile of cheer. And lo! that tear of Pity quenched the flame whereon it fell, and, with the sunshine of that smile, hope entered into hell!

Two unveiled faces full of joy looked upward to the Throne, four white wings folded at the feet of Him who sat thereon!

And deeper than the sound of seas,
more soft than falling flake, amidst the hush
of wing and song the Voice Eternal spake:

"Welcome, my angels! ye have brought a
holier joy to heaven; henceforth its sweetest
song shall be the song of sin forgiven!"

JOHN GREENLEAF WHITTIER

It's food too fine for angels;
yet come take
And eat thy fill!
It's Heaven's sugar cake.

EDWARD TAYLOR

With silence only as their benediction
God's angels come where,
in the shadow of a great affliction
The soul sits dumb.

JOHN GREENLEAF WHITTIER

Tongues of Men and Angels

If I speak in the tongues of men and of angels, but have not love, I am only a resounding gong or a clanging cymbal. If I have the gift of prophecy and can fathom all mysteries and all knowledge, and if I have a faith that can move mountains, but have not love, I am nothing. If I give all I possess to the poor and surrender my body to the flames, but have not love, I gain nothing.

1 CORINTHIANS 13:1-3

Made for Thee

Made for Thyself, O God! made for
Thy love, Thy service, Thy delight;
made to show forth Thy wisdom, grace and
might; made for Thy praise, whom veiled
archangels love; oh, strange and glorious
thought, that we may be a joy to Thee!

FRANCES R. HAVERGAL

I love to hear the story which angel voices tell.

EMILY MILLER

*It is not because angels are holier than men
or devils that makes them angels, but because
they do not expect holiness from one another,
but from God alone.*

WILLIAM BLAKE

The Divine Lullaby

I hear Thy voice, dear Lord; I hear it by
the stormy sea when winter nights are black
and wild, and when, affright, I call to Thee;
it calms my fears and whispers me,
"Sleep well, my child."

I hear Thy voice, dear Lord, in singing winds, in
falling snow, the curfew chimes, the midnight
bell. "Sleep well, my child," it murmurs low;
"The guardian angels come and go,
— O child, sleep well!"

I hear Thy voice, dear Lord, ay, though the
singing winds be stilled, though hushed the
tumult of the deep, my fainting heart with anguish
chilled by Thy assuring tone is thrilled,—
"Fear not, and sleep!"

Speak on—speak on, dear Lord! and when
the last dread night is near, with doubts and
fears and terrors wild, oh, let my soul expiring
hear only these words of heavenly cheer,
"Sleep well, my child!"

EUGENE FIELD

In pity angels beheld Him and came from the world of light, to comfort Him in the sorrows He bore for my soul that night.

CHARLES H. GABRIEL

To wish to act like angels while we are still in this world is nothing but folly.

TERESA OF AVILA

Keep on loving each other as brothers. Do not forget to entertain strangers, for by so doing some people have entertained angels without knowing it.

HEBREWS 13:1-2

Sometimes on lonely mountain-meres
I find a magic bark; I leap on board: no
helmsman steers: I float till all is dark. A
gentle sound, an awful light! Three angels bear
the holy Grail: with folded feet, in stoles of
white, on sleeping wings they sail. Ah,
blessed vision! blood of God! My spirit beats
her mortal bars, as down dark tides the glory
slides, and star-like mingles with the stars.

ALFRED, LORD TENNYSON

"Angel" is the only word in the language which can never be worn out.

VICTOR HUGO

Angel of God, my Guardian dear, to whom God's love entrusts me here; ever this day be at my side, to light and guard, to rule and guide.

TRADITIONAL PRAYER

Unless you can love, as the angels may,

With the breadth of heaven betwixt you;

Unless you can dream that his faith is fast,

Through behoving and unbehoving;

Unless you can die when the dream is past—

Oh, never call it loving!

ROBERT BROWNING

*Hail, Guardian Angels of the House! Come
to our aid, share with us our work and play.
Be with us that we may hear your wings,
and feel your breath upon our cheek.*

GEOFFREY HODSON

*Tis only when they spring to Heaven that
angels reveal themselves to you.*

ROBERT BROWNING

Reflections of Light

Angels are intelligent reflections of light, that original light which has no beginning. They can illuminate. They do not need tongues or ears, for they can communicate without speech, in thought.... They are limited in their powers: when in Heaven they cannot be on earth at the same time, and when God sends them to earth, they cannot remain in Heaven at the same time.

Yet they are not captive to walls and doors;
in this respect they are unlimited. When
God sends them to appear to good men, they do
not reveal themselves in their true shape,
but in a changed semblance that men can see....
As disembodied mind, they live in a mental cli-
mate and are not limited as bodies are.
They do not need the three dimensions. Wherever
they are sent, they are there as mind and
there can take on power, but they cannot do this
in more than one place at a time.

The Angel that presided o'er my birth
Said, "Little creature, formed of joy
and mirth, go love without the help
of any thing on earth."

WILLIAM BLAKE

When one that holds communion with the skies

Has fill'd his urn where these pure waters rise,

And once more mingles with us meaner things,

'Tis e'en as if an angel shook his wings.

William Cowper

Out yonder in the moonlight,

wherein God's Acre lies,

Go angels walking to and fro,

singing their lullabies.

Their radiant wings are folded,

and their eyes are bended low,

As they sing among the beds

whereon the flowers delight to grow.

EUGENE FIELD

Azrael

*The angels in high places who minister to us,
reflect God's smile, their faces are luminous; save
one, whose face is hidden, (The Prophet saith).
The unwelcome, the unbidden. Azrael, Angel of
Death. And yet that veiled face, I know is lit
with pitying eyes, like those faint stars, the first
to glow through cloudy winter skies.*

That they may never tire, Angels, by God's decree, bear wings of snow and fire—passion and purity; save one, all unavailing, (The Prophet saith), His wings are gray and trailing, Azrael, Angel of Death. And yet the souls that Azrael brings across the dark and cold, look up beneath those folded wings, and find them lined with gold.

ROBERT GILBERT WALSH

We live and love—
in the presence of angels.